THIS WINDOW MAKES ME FEEL

Robert Fitterman

Thanks to the editors and publishers of *Brooklyn Rail*, *PomPom*, *Arras*, and *Filling Station* where parts of this text first appeared. An online version of this text was published in the ubu Editions digital book series (2004), and an excerpt of this text was published in *Rob the Plagiarist* (Roof Books, 2009).

ISBN 978-1-937027-95-7
First Edition, First Printing, 2018
Edition of two thousand copies

Ugly Duckling Presse
The Old American Can Factory
232 Third Street #E-303
Brooklyn, NY 11215
www.uglyducklingpresse.org

Distributed in the USA by SPD/Small Press Distribution
Distributed in the UK by Inpress Books
Distributed in Canada by Raincoast Books via Coach House Books

Design and typesetting by Don't Look Now!
The type is Bell Gothic Std
Covers printed letterpress at Ugly Duckling Presse
Foil-stamping by Hodgins Engraving
Offset printing and binding by McNaughton & Gunn
Cover paper donated by Materials for the Arts

Funding for this book was provided, in part, by the National Endowment for the Arts, by public funds from the New York City Department of Cultural Affairs in partnership with the City Council, and by the continued support of the New York State Council on the Arts.

THIS WINDOW MAKES ME FEEL

New York City - 8:35 AM, September 11, 2001

This window makes me feel like I'm protected. This window makes me feel like people don't know much about recent history, at least as far as trivia goes. This window makes me feel whole and emotionally satisfied. This window makes me feel like I'm flying all over the place, gliding and swirling down suddenly. This window makes me feel like I count and I enjoy knowing my opinions are heard so that hopefully I can help change the future. This window makes me feel like I'll find the one thing that makes me feel like I want to feel. This window makes me feel like I can tackle any problem anytime. This window makes me feel like I have energy again and it refreshes my brain cells and makes my feet move. This window makes me feel like I'm the only person who can do something as cool as drumming. This window makes me feel like it's better to hear that other people have gone through it—it's like a rainbow at the end of the storm. This window makes me feel good and grounded and peaceful all at the same time. This window makes me feel like the year I spent campaigning was worth it. This window makes me feel like the artist really knows something about the truth. This window makes me feel really good and also makes me feel like it heightens the sex when it finally happens. This window makes me feel like I'm walking along a creek behind a supermarket. The window makes me feel like I did when I went to a heavy-metal hair stylist who wore a swastika belt buckle and I didn't say anything.

This window makes me feel like violence is around every corner. This window makes me feel like there is a part of the news story that I missed. This window makes me feel like I'm a rabbit being hunted. This window makes me feel like I have a tangible, relevant role in some ongoing process. This window makes me feel like I've won a prize, like I got a part in a movie. This window makes me feel like I do when I hug my dog. This window makes me feel like I want to travel there and find out for myself. This window makes me feel like a special person to have them take a personal interest in my life. This window makes me feel like I'm on the ship in *Ben-Hur*. This window makes me feel so uncomfortable like when people judge other people's sexuality. This window makes me feel like I'm giving back something to the place that gives so much to me. This window makes me feel like I've always been somebody outside looking in. This window makes me feel more Jewish. This window makes me feel like I do when I take care of other people. This window makes me feel like people rely on me to get the job done. This window makes me feel like she's a nice girl who makes mistakes. This window makes me feel like it's raining outside and I feel dizzy and I like it. This window makes me feel blessed that I will be living in America for another year. This window makes me feel weird like I know what happened on that visit couldn't happen and it makes me feel good to see how things have changed for the better. This window makes me feel good about myself to be able to paint because my artwork helps me to show my feelings that I couldn't show before. This window makes me feel like I cannot be responsible for what other people say or do. This window makes me feel rich as I engage in this non-essential and expensive habit. This window makes me feel good to know that my company cares enough about its employees to even consider going for a program like this. This window makes me feel good knowing that the little things that I do can make such a positive difference in others' lives. This window makes me feel like I really shouldn't take extensive lie-ins on Sundays, that I've wasted most of the day, which makes me feel like I'm cheating. This

window makes me feel more mature like when I volun-
teered at the hospital. This window makes me feel good
and lets me know that I'm a pretty good player. This
window makes me feel like my disappointment is a rock
in my chest—it makes me feel hard inside. This window
makes me feel like I'm actually doing some good and
besides I get to sneak in a lesson on life. This window
makes me feel like I have knocked down some pretty
thick walls for others. This window makes me feel like
I have a front row seat at the world's most ancient and
mysterious show, that I am witness to the dawn of time.
This window makes me feel unwanted and ugly and
sometimes it makes me feel dirty when we make love
because I don't know what he's thinking about. This

window makes me feel rich but what a contradiction because I loathe capitalist hullabaloo yet still crave Vegas. This window makes me feel closer to God by worshiping through song. This window makes me feel my loneliness more keenly. This window makes me feel weird and I feel like people are looking at me and that makes me nervous. This window makes me feel like I need to go behind his back when I want to spend money. This window makes me feel like a man and nothing else has ever made me feel like a man. This window makes me feel like he's perfect no matter how mad he makes me. This window makes me feel almost as good as diving does because I'm online about 10 hours a day—I have very, very, very few real life friends—I'm pathetic. This window makes me feel like stupidity comes from the inside. This window makes me feel like I did when I was walking down the street one day and I met a perfect stranger who said that he was on his way to becoming a Ranger. This window makes me feel like I need to learn how to play a musical instrument using an instructional video course. This window makes me feel good to know that we are being protected by the owner here. This window makes me feel like, well, really stupid, and going back and looking at it makes me feel doubly stupid. This window makes me feel like I hate doing anything alone—I can't go to a restaurant and drink a cup of coffee in a café alone, shop alone, etc. This window makes me feel like I have been using hairpieces for the past nine years. This window makes me feel like I need to lie down and take a break. This window makes me feel good inside and sometimes that's what's important. This window makes me feel all tingly inside because I was just nominated for an award. This window makes me feel like the many nights when my sister and I left our bunk beds and camped out on the living room floor. This window makes me feel like it must be the adrenaline that pumps into my system when I rush that makes me so exhausted and stressed. This window makes me feel like I'm sticking way out in front and people actually stare quite blatantly at my belly which makes me feel freakish and shy. This window makes me feel like I'm in a Jacuzzi.

This window makes me feel really happy that you decided to call me yourself. This window makes me feel like I do on sunny days laying down in my bed and listening to soft music — like having a home of my own. This window makes me feel like a bag of sunflower seeds. This window makes me feel like words simply can't express how awesome this is. This window makes me feel like I have a bird's eye view as I perch on the commander's seat looking out the overhead window and maybe seeing another spacecraft in proximity. This window makes me feel powerful the way poetry does, or the poster I saw in a store window. This window makes me feel like I enjoy napping on the sunny floor, pouncing on a toy and eating tasty treats — if I come to a website that makes me feel uncomfortable, I leave it right away. This window makes me feel like I'm underwater. This window makes me feel like I end up with nothing, but somehow it makes me feel better. This window makes me feel like I have the best of city lifestyle, with coffee shops and boutiques right outside my door. This window makes me feel like I am progressing, bettering my work, and it's something that I can take with me. This window makes me feel like the sun is touching my skin and I close my eyes and get sleepy. This window makes me feel like why should I wait for him to do it to me when I can do it to him first. This window makes me feel uneasy like I'm at a ticket counter. This window makes me feel like I might have been really depressed by it three years ago, but now it just seems silly. This window makes me feel like the said medicine has kicked in a 'lil and I feel good enough to type without going off on feverish tangents. This window makes me feel like a fool because when he sings, my wife puts her arms around the radio. This window makes me feel like a mass of flesh cuddles and strokes me under my skin. This window makes me feel nostalgic for things I've never done. This window makes me feel like our little circle can watch them while they're at school. This window makes me feel like what doesn't kill me will make me stronger. This window makes me feel great to think that I started this field from scratch and now look at it. This window makes me feel like you can't barge into my little world. This window makes me feel like I'm looking at a flat industrial wasteland and I'm glad I get to see some wide, open spaces. This window makes me feel like I should be wrapped up in a blanket as I listen to the sounds of water falling. This window makes me feel like I'm making myself sick over what happened and it could be so easily changed. This window makes me feel more or less like I'm drifting in space, or actually like I'm racing with space. This window makes me feel like locking the door. This window makes me feel like I get my love of nature from my dad. This window makes me feel like we are almost parallel and that makes me feel more comfortable. This window makes me feel the glow and it brightens up my world.

This window makes me feel like I am trembling with fear because normally I'm a heavy-sleeper. This window makes me feel numb and skeptical about most everything. This window makes me feel like I'm watching a runner and she wants me to cross that river. This window makes me feel satisfied to know that I've reached a lot of people. This window makes me feel like he isn't interested or he's just bored because all he does is sleep or watch TV — he doesn't hardly ever talk to me. This window makes me feel like I'm cheating because I've been intimate with an old boyfriend online. This window makes me feel like he's choosing to go on a date with her instead of just stopping her from hurting me. This window makes me feel like my current

17

generation is too often described in ways to imply that we need to be fixed or corrected. This window makes me feel like an even bigger goober because I didn't get my license until I was 22. This window makes me feel like I'm the source of the problem and it makes me feel sad and guilty. This window makes me feel like a loser and the fact that I don't drink coffee or drive a stick only makes things worse. This window makes me feel like the craftsman I am whenever I wear it and people comment on it. This window makes me feel like she's lying when she says she's only reached it twice and we've been together for two years and she says only twice. This window makes me feel like I have a really extended family, both here and in Thailand, who cares for me. This window makes me feel like the most spoiled woman in America. This window makes me feel like a better person and it all started with my desire to teach others what I know. This window makes me feel like some kind of second-class global citizen living in a second-rate country. This window makes me feel like I'm scouring shops in SoHo and Tribeca even though I live in a small, historical town, so access to these kinds of products is usually limited. This window makes me feel like I'm still in the loop. This window makes me feel like his parents don't trust our relationship because they made this condition that the house would be in his name only. This window makes me feel like shit, although that little fact continues to be invisible to the people who should be seeing it very clearly. This window makes me feel like an idiot because I need my mother to think that I look like one, too. This window makes me feel like a huge geek largely because I was never a cartoon fan before. This window makes me feel like something must be wrong or that he isn't satisfied with me even though I used to think our sex life was great. This window makes me feel like a dancer even though I don't have a dancer's build. This window makes me feel like I am worth something because they respect my ideas and treat me just like one of them. This window makes me feel like something of a heel but, damn it, someone has to say something. This window makes me feel like a fool because I spent a lot of time trying to get the password to work and told a lot of friends about it. This window makes me feel like the quintessential mod from *Quadrophenia*. This window makes me feel like I am looking out of a cell and wishing I could return to therapy. This window makes me feel like a genuine rebel as I listen to some punk rock anarchistic lament on my Walkman. This window makes me feel like an evil person, and it saddens me, but at the same time, we can't change what we feel. This window makes me feel like it's one step forward and two steps back, thereby severely limiting my business's net growth. This window makes me feel like I'm worth absolutely nothing as I wonder what else they've been covering up. This window makes me feel like a curmudgeon, and, besides, it's hard to stay up late for the real craziness if you're not chemically altered. This window makes me feel like my time and experience are not important to the education system here. This window makes me feel like a card-carrying member of the Family of Man. This window makes me feel like I need to pay more attention. This window makes me feel like I am losing my identity as a Southerner—all too often I find myself buying gas at BP and not Jake's. This window makes me feel like I am going in slow motion. This window makes me feel like a winner against seedy merchants who only care about a profit. This window makes me feel like if I did have to serve in the military, it would be for a good reason and not for some faraway vague cause. This window makes me feel like I'm not making enough money to be independent even though I can say that I am happy being at home and I am comfortable enough. This window makes me feel like I'm the root of the problem. This window makes me feel badly talking about this, plus I realize I've made some other people feel sad and weird. This window makes me feel like I have to walk on eggshells with him so that I don't get on his nerves. This window makes me feel pretty badly because you dismiss me with a flick of your hand like I'm a peasant, and you think it's funny. This window makes me feel like I'm rushing into an uncertain future when my girlfriend talks about getting married, and she talks about it such a lot. This window makes me feel like my trust was wasted on you—can you explain this to me? This window makes me feel like I have an inferiority complex, like I know people are definitely better than me at dancing, singing, and various other things. This window makes me feel like I have to spend more time checking grammar and spelling, and that I wish I had learned more about English in school. This window makes me feel like abstaining when the only choices are Republican and Democrat. This window makes me feel like I whine way too much about the guys I wish I could have but can't—it's just so frustrating. This window makes me feel like I have to go wash my hands—excuse me. This window makes me feel like such an inadequate person—I feel like I screw everything up and can't do anything right. This window makes me feel like it's hard sometimes to bring our inner feelings out into words. This window makes me feel like I live in LA and I'm a struggling actor or something. This window makes me feel like I'm in a hole of absolute shit-ness and abyss. This window makes me feel like people really care and I can get things off my mind and this helps me gain my sanity in this insane world. This window makes me feel like such a cheese ball, though when am I not? This window makes me feel like I lead such a boring life that I don't even know what I would do to make it less boring. This window makes me feel like a failure because when I don't attend my classes my grades drop and I fall behind and I know I may not graduate. This window makes me feel like an absolute amateur—I really can't compete—but I'll keep trying. This window makes me feel like it is not actually a cohesive piece of writing, but something that more resembles a laundry list. This window makes me feel like I got roaches crawling in my stomach and I can't do anything on my own. This window makes me feel like the slowdown will be short because there are still some inventories out there, but not nearly what we've seen in the past. This window makes me feel like there was a moment today that was like a dagger through my heart. This window makes me feel a little sad, since part of my journey to Boston was a personal search for liberation. This window makes me feel real uneasy—look, I don't know old you are, but I'm assuming you're in high school. This window makes me feel the most lost and the most together—I mean, are my parents really so different from families that aren't divorced? This window makes me feel like immediately blaming the selfishness of my mother, but there is a larger issue here. This window makes me feel like we ought to enforce laws against scalping tickets and other black market operations. This window makes me feel like I must be crazy to continue to sit next to this psycho. This window makes me feel very angry because it's a terrible waste of this country's talent and resources. This window makes me feel like I did the right thing by pouring the bottles down the drain as he stood in total disbelief. This window makes me feel like I want to sharpen my skills that much more to get to where I want to be. This window makes me feel weighted down, lost, and afraid, but maybe I'm overly concerned about change or transitions because I'm changing jobs or career orientation. This window makes me feel like the temporary situation of living in a small apartment sometimes makes my husband and I go crazy because both of us like reading and we're home a lot. This window makes me feel like the only reason I am going to say "why me" is to find out what I can do to make the situation better. This window makes me feel like laughing, even though it was one of the worst mistakes in my life, looking at it from today's perspective. This window makes me feel sick because I need to be alone but I can't stand being on my own—my mind is so full of conflicts. This window makes me feel like they don't know much about careers or personality types—please, someone write a real MBTI career-counseling book. This window makes me feel like I did when I was young and my mother would spell something out for my father, or my sister and her girlfriends would talk on their own in secret whispers. This window makes me feel like I have been taking care of myself since I was 12 years old when I got the boot from mom and dad. This window makes me feel sad for many reasons, but I don't want people to think I'm going to hell—that's between me and God. This window makes me feel outraged...

after all, I don't need the credit card... my track record has proved that I'm a poor manager of credit, okay? This window makes me feel nervous because he has been on medication lately but he hasn't been getting any professional help. This window makes me feel like I don't have my head on straight—I don't know, the idea kind of appeals/appealed to me which I suppose is strange. This window makes me feel like I need a summer job to hold me over until the fall. This window makes me feel like reflecting on the mountain bike community and the ripple effect—for me, I never had a problem with hunters or trappers. This window makes me feel like I'm having some strange mental problem. This window makes me feel uncomfortable and I know he's uncomfortable, too—because of his age, he cannot be moved to another division. This window makes me feel like what a bubble we all live in and what is the world coming to. This window makes me feel like a wrench has been shoved into my chest and turned around and around. This window makes me feel like maybe I'm not the self-assured, confident person I think I am because I feel like an idiot for not being able to handle this situation. This window makes me feel like these solutions are better than they imagine and that has seriously reduced my stress level. This window makes me feel like it might not even be legal for his employer to fire him, and it might even be a violation of the Americans with Disabilities Act. This window makes me feel like canceling the rest of my order due to the shabbiness of the whole situation, even though I have been an excellent customer in the past. This window makes me feel excluded and it's just wrong that it's being held in a private home and not everyone in the community is welcome. This window makes me feel like a groupie but not, I hope, a dishonest one—my only real agenda is to bring awareness into the American consciousness. This window makes me feel like how many parents and teens see no connection between God's word preached on Sunday and the decisions they make during the week. This window makes me feel like the taboo goes too far in not allowing for exceptions. This window makes me feel like I'm immersed in reality and it's a good thing that I can still dream and fly. This window makes me feel like it's payback time. This window makes me feel young like when my mother used to touch my cheek to check for fever, or praise me, or brush my hair out of my eyes, and there was that special scent. This window makes me feel like dressing up, which is the one thing I loved as a kid and still do. This window makes me feel, like, bad about all the bragging I did to my friends at the time. This window makes me feel like I have that what-did-I-tell-you cynic sound in my voice. This window makes me feel unclean; maybe I need a shower, which is a good idea. This window makes me feel homesick, if you can call it that, like a family picture on the beach and the kids are snorkeling. This window makes me feel angry — if you don't have enough money you are poor, as ex-President Grover Cleveland would say. This window makes me feel like I have to go in between an old prickly bush and a rugged brick wall, in order to touch the impermeable glass of her ground-level apartment. This window makes me feel like I just ran a vacuum cleaner across the carpet a few times. This window makes me feel like these people are too real to be actors. This window makes me feel like I wouldn't be caught dead wearing one of those things on my head. This window makes me feel like I am essentially shamanistic; for whatever reason, the drug rejected me. This window makes me feel like just walking away because I didn't mean to make you blush. This window makes me feel like the room has an entirely different feel to it now and the mural makes it a fun place to work. This window makes me feel like the sound squirrels make when you chase them away from the bird feeder. This window makes me feel like I have impeccable taste in music. This window makes me feel like his version of multiculturalism makes me want to gesture at the deluge outside. This window makes me feel like I'm looking at Bombay and I'm thinking of my friends and family. This window makes me feel like I'm in a time machine, way in the future. This window makes me feel like I can feel the mushrooms popping out of my pores. This window makes me feel like buying that new scarf was an extra little purchase just to make my day. This window makes me feel like religion is important because it makes some kind of metaphysical bridge even though I grew up in a completely secular household. This window makes me feel like nothing is mine—even the wristwatch I'm wearing was given to me. This window makes me feel like I'm sitting in the back seat of a nappy yellow Buick. This window makes me feel like I'm being tortured with the sun beating down on me. This window makes me feel like I'm coming home to a house of dirty dishes. This window makes me feel they are letting me into a family music gathering—very pleasant indeed! This window makes me feel like I am traveling to their country without taking an airplane. This window makes me feel like, hello, was the word DUMB tattooed on my forehead or not. This window makes me feel like the ending makes me shiver with tingly delight. This window makes me feel like what I do doesn't really matter to anyone except other designers. This window makes me feel like I'm wasting perfectly good fruit and this annoys the thou-shall-not-waste-food portion of my soul. This window makes me feel like I will die in my sleep or something. This window makes me feel like I am looking or listening through a retro-filter, but I like its direct authenticity. This window makes me feel like I am nothing but an object, an anonymous female figure to view. This window makes me feel like maybe if I am wrong I'll still have an "in" with the Big Guy because apparently God has trouble seeing through charades. This window makes me feel like I'm coming down with a cold. This window makes me feel like I'm out on the range somewhere or hangin' around the corral because I don't get out as much as I would like to, so I read a lot of cowboy poetry. This window makes me feel like such a weak Christian and a hypocrite, especially when I read the Gospel and witness the perfection of the way Jesus lived. This window makes me feel like a slacker—good thing I'm okay with that. This window makes me feel like a romantic morning waking up to the one I love awaiting the morning sun. This window makes me feel it's a dictatorship and I don't see any way of getting rid of the city manager. This window makes me feel like a four-star general with the power I'm gonna have. This window makes me feel like I'll lose a day's pay (maybe two or three). This window makes me feel like my boyfriend is more worried about losing her than he is about losing me. This window makes me feel like my job as a baker is half done. This window makes me feel like I'm back in my first year of college in the dorm: "OK, my name is so-and-so, I'm from here-and-there, my major is something-or-other." This window makes me feel like I should own by now because there's a lot of real-estate going around here recently. This window makes me feel like I'm sliding off the ends. This window makes me feel like I am on a deserted island where I could only communicate by writing a note, putting it in a bottle and waiting for a reply the same way. This window makes me feel like tiny things are beautiful, that there's humor in the industrial world, and that you can go slightly psycho and that will be even truer. This window makes me feel like I am getting to something that I want to expel from my body. This window makes me feel like I'm living in the futuristic world of 1999. This window makes me feel like a total outcast, and it doesn't help that one of the only virgins I know had sex a couple of months ago. This window makes me feel like an old lady because, after all, I am only a creep in my imagination—in real life I am very nice and unthreatening. This window makes me feel like such a slacker because she was only nineteen when she wrote and sang this. This window makes me feel like a violated schoolboy—all members of organized religions that are evil should know the feeling. This window makes me feel like I am a person in one of the cells of a panopticon. This window makes me feel like someone just stepped on my tender spot. This window makes me feel like I can get through anything. This window makes me feel like we should all take the time to stop and smell the flowers. This window makes me feel like I can visit my heritage without even being there. This window makes me feel like they were excited with this project for nine months, and now I can do anything. This window makes me feel like I'm gliding through the water at warp speed and I picture myself in the Olympics racing for the Gold. This window makes me feel like getting piss ass drunk—maybe I will because it's been a long time. This window makes me feel like I did something right for once—listen, I know these people and they will tell you if it's good or bad. This window makes me feel like I'm hearing the names of these plants for the first time. This window makes me feel like a fake because when I handed in the papers I knew what I'd written was far from good. This window makes me feel like I'm still in the "loop" because I've been subbing for a year, but I miss teaching in my own room. This window makes me feel like I'm going and lying down in a darkened room. This window makes me feel like I'm preventing accidents—I take my job seriously even if I joke that there's a downside. This window makes me feel like a bad person because I do second-level technical support for them when I know I could do more. This window makes me feel like you're trying to act like you had nothing to do with it. This window makes me feel like visiting Vietnam some day because I am very interested in the history, the war and peace, and the relationship between the two countries. This window makes me feel like me or one of my friends could be president some day. This window makes me feel like a stupid idiot because I know there may be many people who needed a fraction of my knowledge and experience to get the same results. This window makes me feel like they are taking chances with my life, as my safety will depend on the security personnel making the correct choices. This window makes me feel like I should rinse out my eyes with saline solution for a week. This window makes me feel like kicking some ass. This window makes me feel like *Alice in Wonderland*—I simply cannot go with the dualistic approach. This window makes me feel like I have a popcorn kernel stuck in the back of my throat. This window makes me feel like a freak because I'm probably the only 30-year-old virgin in America who isn't a priest, monk, etc. This window makes me feel like a fossil because the field has changed enormously in these past decades. This window makes me feel like a stalker —I need to calm down—but maybe next semester we can get to know one another. This window makes me feel like I've really accomplished something, and I must have touched a lot of hearts with my writing. This window makes me feel like a bitch, which I hate, but I'm not liking being ignored and I'm not liking the feeling that I need to be validated to be noticed by people. This window makes me feel like I belong, and I am loved, because God wants to be with me. This window makes me feel like I understand a bit more about what makes them tick. This window makes me feel like they really care about my opinion and I'm treated like everyone else is treated. This window makes me feel like a self-centered freak. This window makes me feel like the country mouse when I look back at my hometown in Wichita. This window makes me feel like more of a part of a dream, and fulfilling what God has planned for us in the future. This window makes me feel like they're really listening to me, even when they do most of the talking, and it's a real turn-on. This window makes me feel like I'm handling items in microgravity without changing my orientation. This window makes me feel like I'm not free to say what I want to say. This window makes me feel like I live in the woods. This window makes me feel a bit shaken up—I sleep with the window open, even in winter, with a loaded rifle and a flashlight handy. This window makes me feel like saying, "Please, girl, stick it out with me... I feel a change coming over me." This window makes me feel more

cocky and powerful when I have a good breakfast—
don't eat anything you can buy from a place with a
drive-thru window. This window makes me feel like, I
don't know, it just makes sense to me—it's just my per-
spective. This window makes me feel unhip, out-of-
touch, old, and I don't care if they are the latest fash-
ion or on whose runway they were first spotted. This
window makes me feel like I wish I could get up on the
roof of my apartment building, but there's a revolving
restaurant up there so no way. This window makes me
feel like something of a ''pure scientist'' and, therefore,
one of the very people that I often criticize. This win-
dow makes me feel like he is explicating her position as
a post-linguistic-turned-Kantian position. This window

makes me feel like what happened to me—only a few years ago I was against the old "eye for an eye" thing. This window makes me feel like you could almost smell the sea. This window makes me feel like this will be the last time you'll ever hear from me. This window makes me feel like I could climb a castle wall and you could be Rapunzel, letting your hair down for me. This window makes me feel like no one else thinks about these things. This window makes me feel like there must be a big neon sign on my neck that says "come on over here and hit me." This window makes me feel like we could forget about our own agendas and get ready to get sold. This window makes me feel like I don't know you people, why are you here? This window makes me feel like when I talk badly about their father — it's terrible and it makes me feel torn apart. This window makes me feel inferior because I don't have the flashy clothes that the people in this ad have. This window makes me feel joyful because the sky turns from a beautiful light blue to dark blue. This window makes me feel better about losing stuff at home. This window makes me feel worse about myself because I want so much for people to like me for me, yet I am told by my own husband that I act immature and inappropriate at times. This window makes me feel guilty because we've had far too much rain this year, and farmers like my mother's brother are really suffering. This window makes me feel like all of my education is for nothing and I don't know when I will ever get the right job. This window makes me feel like I am special and loved—when we do nice things for each other we feel happier and want to be together more. This window makes me feel less like a customer and more like a part of the team without talking computerese and without being talked down to. This window makes me feel like I'm a believer in total experience so how do I make peace here? This window makes me feel like the best part of the whole deal is that I don't have any accidents in my pants like I used to. This window makes me feel like the inside is already a man, and I need to make the outside so. This window makes me feel neglected because he says he doesn't believe he needs to participate in these manufactured holidays. This window makes me feel even more alone than before with so many people checking up on me lately. This window makes me feel like he is just completely bitter without having any real human feeling behind it. This window makes me feel an admittedly bizarre and psychologically twisted but loving kinship, like we've been joined unknowingly for the past decade. This window makes me feel like sometimes I see a guy on TV and compare myself to him. This window makes me feel conspicuous in a way that I hadn't expected. This window makes me feel like I'm in Disneyland—my checkbook is balanced, the porch is swept, the plants have been watered, and almost all of my clothes have been put away. This window makes me feel better because I know I covered my ass. This window makes me feel sad because it reveals how melancholically beautiful England is, suburbs and all. This window makes me feel like I need to get a larger gold fish bowl or they're going to keep dying on me. This window makes me feel like I will reach total freedom. This window makes me feel like a heel because I know I am an insecure attention-seeker who has a deep need for total strangers to notice my existence for a very short while. This window makes me feel somewhat better as I can sense that it isn't just me that seems to be getting less than decent service. This window makes me feel sick, but I have to smile and tell you how happy I am for you. This window makes me feel more successful and more prepared to face my future—something which used to scare me when I thought about it. This window makes me feel slightly depressed because there's no food in the house. This window makes me feel like we belong some place and it makes me feel like we've achieved something. This window makes me feel like I perform better when I frequent the gym and feel that I'm working towards a goal. This window makes me feel engulfed in pride and nostalgia. This window makes me feel like if everyone has an American flag it helps spread the pride. This window makes me feel like I'm having a panic attack where my thoughts are racing and I can't breathe very well. This window makes me feel a little better about the fact that I don't have a clue where I'll be next year. This window makes me feel like I'm looking at mountains even though there aren't any mountains for miles and miles. This window makes me feel like so normal, like I'm glad I'm not jumping into anything. This window makes me feel better because I didn't get an upset collections manager in response to the situation. This window makes me feel at peace because I know that love, through me, has helped show a path that makes things easier. This window makes me feel like I just went over the moon, on a rampage, knocking over around ten other clubbers, causing three to lose consciousness. This window makes me feel a little uneasy like he's capitalizing on the tragedy. This window makes me feel alive as I look up at the skies, take a deep breath, and look at the stars shining bright up there. This window makes me feel like no matter who I am and what I've done, I do have a chance. This window makes me feel like everyone around me is giving the two-thumbs-up sign. This window makes me feel guilty, of course, so I don't indulge in the fantasy for too long. This window makes me feel more in control of what needs to be done, and it makes it easier for me to structure my day. This window makes me feel like the anger's building because I don't care what you do anymore, and you obviously don't care how I feel. This window makes me feel like I'm testing shampoo on a bald man. This window makes me feel like telling someone how much I love his or her product, which is very soothing and effective. This window makes me feel a little bit like each spring when I find myself coupled with some newfound mate. This window makes me feel like I must be so unimportant to him if he tells me he was busy all day and that he didn't even have the chance to call me until late at night. This window makes me feel very insecure about my manhood, what with the pink artwork and the fucking unicorn on the front. This window makes me feel like I am in someone's fantasy. This window makes me feel like I don't have his full attention and that he'd rather not be talking to me, which is plenty annoying. This window makes me feel more comfortable and relaxed with my surroundings because we treat each other casually by calling everyone by their first names. This window makes me feel like trash and like everyone thinks I'm trashy being big on top and having to look like this. This window makes me feel a lot better because (A) it gives me hope that maybe he will quit soon, and (B) I figure that if they haven't fired him after all that shit then I don't know what. This window makes me feel totally awkward, like I'm the only single person in the club — it's crowded and I can barely move without hitting someone. This window makes me feel like I should go back to bed and read some more mystery novels. This window makes me feel like I'm looking out on a positive horizon; it was hard but I asked for a bit of leeway and so far I have not been late at all. This window makes me feel very insecure, not only about myself but about us as a couple, knowing that she does not like me as much as she likes women. This window makes me feel very optimistic about the future of Latino entertainment. This window makes me feel significant in the big man circles, but I've learned that I am just a presentable prop for pompous occasions such as this one. This window makes me feel like I'm a little bit more at home because in approximately one hour we will be told who is going where and doing what. This window makes me feel like I'm coming home to a warm cottage in the middle of a cornfield, gentle guitars. This window makes me feel very excited, walking outside only wearing a short towel — I walk past a lot of people and I enjoy this. This window makes me feel like life is worth living, which I sure need after having to deal with a bunch of characters like you all year. This window makes me feel like a complete fraud as I preach to my workshop participants about how they have the ability to live their dreams. This window makes me feel like I'm in high demand and that's all the motivation I need to sit down and organize my thoughts. This window makes me feel like a chicken-and-egg problem. This window makes me feel like one of those old white guys on the porch talking about hanging people and how everyone is a commie pinko. This window makes me feel like I'm reading the same story over again, but with an unlikely plot and a disappointing character.

This window makes me feel like we accomplished a lot more on the other days when the downtime is at a high. This window makes me feel like no one wants to answer my personal, especially when it's been viewed over 30 plus times and not one reply. This window makes me feel damn lost and empty so I turn to cigarettes, which give me a high, and I feel pretty good. This window makes me feel so good about the field trip tomorrow because I'm totally organized and the weather is looking great. This window makes me feel focused on only one thing: to give and receive pleasure without any control, and I'm starting to enjoy this feeling a lot. This window makes me feel like I am looking out over the skyline and forgetting who I am and what I'm supposed to be doing. This window makes me feel like I'm wearing a vault door. This window makes me feel like *Rocky*, Number One, and it means I get to drive the fuck away from the house for awhile with the top down and the music blasting. This window makes me feel like I'm never going to get out of that virtual filing cabinet. This window makes me feel like I am a legitimate writer, and as if the journey is actually going to lead somewhere. This window makes me feel like a miniature Billy Graham. This window makes me feel like a tourist, like I've never seen this view before or something. This window makes me feel like it's a pretty nice day weather-wise. This window makes me feel like a sculptor carving a white, marble statue. This window makes me feel like one of those little birds that picks bugs off of water buffalo. This window makes me feel like a winner—it's only noon and I am so proud to have sold 67 shirts already. This window makes me feel like I'm suffocating—I like a constant influx of fresh air. This window makes me feel like the purple and white lilacs are blooming before my eyes, and the pink dogwood trees are spreading gloriously. This window makes me feel much better about taking off from Reagan National Airport. This window makes me feel joyful because I wanted to get the town below and the sky on top and the water for the base. This window makes me feel like I have no sympathy for Milošević. This window makes me feel as if Jesus is making sure the gateway to heaven stays open. This window makes me feel so uninspired, like morning rain—since the day I started here, life's been so benign. This window makes me feel really charged—I have it in front of me at my workplace and I feel a positive energy when I look at it everyday. This window makes me feel like I love him like a stray pet off the street, but nonetheless I feel my blood pooling on the ground, and I can feel its crimson liquidity forming around me. This window makes me feel like I should remember my emotional self more often, the side of me that somehow seems to get lost. This window makes me feel like I must have had a wonderful breakfast; I think it was mainly the fact that it was warm, and it makes me wanna rush home and prepare it again. This window makes me feel good inside and I want to be able to feel this same thing while taking on the challenges of becoming a sergeant. This window makes me feel like I'm the source of the problem and I don't want the two of them to be mean to each other. This window makes me feel angry because even though I don't want to rehash the funding issue in this month's column, I do feel compelled to address the questions and comments I received. This window makes me feel like I want to die because one false move on my part and I know the whole thing will come crashing down. This window makes me feel mad, sad, anxious, concerned, out of control, and a ton of other emotions. This window makes me feel unsafe and vulnerable being dressed in a top which is not tucked into my track-suit bottoms. This window makes me feel like I have the key to exploring myself. This window makes me feel like a mondo dork — I've mostly recovered my dignity from this self-demoralizing view, but, wow, I'm a huge loser. This window makes me feel like I have a deep peace within my soul, but I'm not suggesting that this makes me a better person, or that I look down upon others. This window makes me feel really old because a kid I grew up with is a candidate for the US Senate this year. This window makes me feel like I want to rob a liquor store just to make ends meet. This window makes me feel like I'm starting to see why people view life experience as a spiral; we keep coming back to the same goddamn realizations. This window makes me feel all tingly inside like when I was walking on the warm sand and playing in the shiny warm water—I'll be back next summer. This window makes me feel invisible, unreal, and it invalidates my feelings as an individual. This window makes me feel like laughing when the city is so bright and right, but it doesn't look beautiful or ugly— it just is. This window makes me feel like I am really special, and I have the best common sense in the world, but also I know how to mediate, how to be diplomatic, and God knows these people could use someone like me. This window makes me feel like I could go back home anytime I wanted to. This window makes me feel like I've messed up everything—not only for myself but for my department too. This window makes me feel like something weird is going on because there are a lot of birds swirling around or circling in on something. This window makes me feel like I'm part of the parade even though I'm up here and have to be at my desk. This window makes me feel like I should learn how to burn my own CDs instead of asking my friends to do it for me. This window makes me feel really confused about what people expect from me—I guess I'll know more when I get a response and I can't believe it's almost five o'clock and I haven't gotten a response yet. This window makes me feel like I was way too impulsive about buying those gifts and I'll probably take most of them back. This window makes me feel really upset

67

about the fact that I'm always the one doing the apologizing—I mean, okay, it's partly my fault but it takes two to tango, don't it? This window makes me feel very badly about the whole Garden Club mix-up. This window makes me feel great about all of the opportunities I'm being presented with. This window makes me feel like I live inside a jackhammer, I can't take it anymore, and it looks like the construction is never going to end. This window makes me feel like my mother doesn't have a clue and I don't even know where I would start with her. This window makes me feel like I missed a meeting or something even though I don't see anything in my planner for today. This window makes me feel like the whole industry is a lot trickier than one might think. This window makes me feel like looking in the Sunday paper and seeing if anyone is running a good furniture sale. This window makes me feel like I'm just walking along a river and I'm thinking, "Oh God, if I could express in a phrase what I feel." This window makes me feel like it's not my fault if the one I love is into porn—talk about signs focusing on behaviors, and observations and reactions to them. This window makes me feel really young again because I'm working on an elk-handled bowie knife from scratch. This window makes me feel really uneasy even though I hate to make performance-based arguments without any code. This window makes me feel so good that I don't mind doing anything that I consider safe, sane, and consensual. This window makes me feel like the smell of fresh summer air, like I'm ready to face the day after nine hours of sleep. This window makes me feel like I am slowly picking up the courage and I'm being sent to different districts to participate in tournaments. This window makes me feel really good, like when my uncle comes to visit and comments on what a nice, clean room I have. This window makes me feel like I'm talking about flight schedules. This window makes me feel like a hopeless thing, like a wandering possibility. This window makes me feel worse because everybody's trying to cheer me up and bombarding me with comfort phrases like, "your speech was awesome," blah blah blah. This window makes me feel extremely

disgusted with the ways of modern medicine that sac-
rifice human life and treat people's bodies as mere ob-
jects. This window makes me feel like when I asked my
mom if this is bad because it makes me feel good, and
she said that it wasn't bad at all and that, in fact, she
sort of liked the feeling herself. This window makes me
feel amazed by how much faster and faster I come
back to my old self. This window makes me feel safe—
after ten years of strutting my stuff, I'm still HIV-free,
and in this kind of setting I've found sex work to be an
absolute joy. This window makes me feel like you can
see something where you say, hey, that's life. This win-
dow makes me feel like I need to pay more attention in
class. This window makes me feel like my own goals

and those of the organization are in line when I talk about pay, promotion, and quality of work. This window makes me feel like I'm looking at a plate-sized moth on his back, the sun setting on the Bon Jovi sweatshirts and Princess Diana tees. This window makes me feel a hundred times more comfortable expressing myself in the future. This window makes me feel good about buying those ornaments — it really says Christmas. This window makes me feel like the chances of ever winning the Lotto are even smaller, I mean, what are the odds of even knowing a winner. This window makes me feel happier when I study mostly because of the multi-colored chairs in the library. This window makes me feel kind of disgusted even though I know that he is entitled to do whatever he wants with himself. This window makes me feel perpetually at peace and totally untouched by the third dimensional energy. This window makes me feel so international, so cosmopolitan, so weirded out now that we have two Au Bon Pains. This window makes me feel relaxed because I'm working with my dad and enjoying every minute of it and I know he has confidence in me as a horse-shoer. This window makes me feel not only unattractive to white men but to black men as well. This window makes me feel wonderful because the ever-present heaviness that had plagued me has now diminished significantly. This window makes me feel like we cannot manage in isolation when conducting ocean-based research. This window makes me feel like I just realized the human contact that the cell phone makes possible. This window makes me feel desperate and alone and like I have to pee. This window makes me feel determined and motivated rather than anxious; it converts the adrenaline from flight to fight. This window makes me feel like I'm living in heaven because I get to do all of my hobbies: first traveling, then shooting for sport, and chatting with people. This window makes me feel like an unemployed useless lump. This window makes me feel guilty like I've committed some horrible crime; the spider never did anything to me. This window makes me feel better when I convince myself that I am not angry with the Lord but with myself. This window makes me feel great; it reminds me of when I was doing lots of exercises and felt good about myself. This window makes me feel like I'm all out of options, that I'm so poor and cheap I think I might cry, but I need new shoes and jeans and shirts and shit real bad. This window makes me feel sick and grossly irresponsible, so I will hunker down and berate myself for a few hours. This window makes me feel a lot better because my big healthy appetite is back. This window makes me feel free, alone, and in harmony with everything around me — God, how lucky birds must be for that! This window makes me feel like going to bed. This window makes me feel very confident, like I'm clued into something that English-only readers wouldn't be. This window makes me feel like

I'm walking along with a time bomb in my chest—talk about anxiety, I'm telling ya. This window makes me feel pretty goofy like there's a part of me that obviously cares but I just don't tend to go there. This window makes me feel like this whole place used to be in some-one's mouth. This window makes me feel free because we are, each of us—the living as much as the dead—so very alone. This window makes me feel positively awful even though I have a plan B, of course, that will put enough money in my hands to survive. This window makes me feel a little hypocritical given that there were several profanities and at least one instance of blas-phemy. This window makes me feel sad and filled with self-loathing to think that it is difficult to exist for two days without cell service. This window makes me feel like something went wrong—in *The Way To Happiness* book it says that you should take care of yourself. This window makes me feel a little bit better but now I'm embarrassed about it and I don't feel like having sex because now I feel like a freak. This window makes me feel strange like I should explain that the photo is way hotter than I am in real life and most days I just wear whatever is on the floor. This window makes me feel like I am on my way down... but I've actually been down this same road before... ohhh, here's that beautiful tree again. This window makes me feel welcomed and appreciated... the owls fly overhead... the sun is setting beautiful turquoise, orange, red, and yellow. This window makes me feel like I am not far away from home at all because I work for a company setting world standards in the telecommunications industry. This window makes me feel increasingly pointless. This window makes me feel like staying here on the balcony with them rather than going back to the party and indulging in some overly-sweet cake. This window makes me feel really good about the fireworks display in the schoolyard because I think this really seems to be a unique West Coast thing. This window makes me feel disrespected and unimportant as I consider myself to be a serious, hard-working, goal-oriented, ambitious person. This window makes me feel like I can see beyond my own problems and start to look into those of the people who live here. This window makes me feel like I need to reconsider my friend group—not the most supportive group when it comes being non-conformist. This window makes me feel like it's impossible to eat healthily when client lunches are happening two or three times a week—I keep saying to myself that I'll start eating better tomorrow, and then tomorrow comes and it's another client lunch with wine and dessert. This window makes me feel like global warming messes with my perception of great weather. This window makes me feel like I can see for miles and miles, which makes me feel nostalgic for my rural home and childhood. This window makes me feel like I have only one thing on my mind, all the time, and everybody knows what it is.